THE MONTH·TO·MONTH
ME

WRITTEN BY
LINDA SCHWARTZ
ILLUSTRATED BY
BEVERLY ARMSTRONG

THE LEARNING WORKS

The purchase of this book entitles the
individual teacher to reproduce copies for use
in the classroom.

The reproduction of any part for an entire
school or school system or for commercial
use is strictly prohibited.

No form of this work may be reproduced
or transmitted or recorded without written
permission from the publisher.

INTRODUCTION

The MONTH-TO-MONTH ME is an exciting and motivating way for students to keep an on-going journal about themselves throughout the school year. The book is divided into sections by months, with four exercises for each month of the school year. The activities are ideally suited for independent seat work or for use at a learning center. Students can make and illustrate folders to keep their pages in as they work. The young authors can then design original covers for their completed book at the end of the school year.

MONTH-TO-MONTH ME provides opportunities for creative thinking, art and creative writing and also gives students a chance to gain a better understanding and insight into themselves. By doing several exercises a month, students will have a meaningful memento by the end of the school year — a book worth saving and reflecting upon both now and in the future.

BE IT KNOWN
TO ALL PEOPLE
THAT

_____

HAS, ON THIS _____ DAY
OF _____, IN
THE YEAR _____
SUCCESSFULLY
COMPLETED ALL PAGES
OF "THE MONTH·TO·
MONTH ME". HURRAH

_____

TEACHER'S SIGNATURE

THE MONTH-TO-MONTH ME

CONTENTS

MY STORY

1. My name is _____ .

2. I live at _____ _____ _____ .
   ADDRESS   CITY   STATE

3. My telephone number is _____ .

4. I am _____ years old. I was born on _____, _____, _____,
                                           DAY   MONTH   YEAR
   in _____ , _____ .
      CITY   STATE

5. I weighed _____ when I was born. I now weigh _____

   and am _____ tall.

6. I have _____ hair and have _____ eyes.
          COLOR   COLOR

7. I do _____ do not _____ wear eye-glasses. (check one)

8. I do _____ do not _____ have freckles. (check one)

I have freckles,
wear eye-glasses,
and am left handed.

9. I am right handed _____ left handed _____ . (check one)

10. I am in the _____ grade at _____ .
                                            NAME OF SCHOOL

11. There are _____ people in my family counting me. They are:

    _____

    _____

My telephone number is 525·630·3580.

A SELF PORTRAIT

This is how I look at the beginning of the school year.

Draw your picture here.

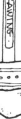

MY HANDWRITING

This is a sample of my best handwriting. I will save it and compare this page with my handwriting at the end of the school year.

COPY THIS PARAGRAPH.

This is a sample of my best handwriting. It is part of a book called **THE MONTH-TO-MONTH ME.** Each month I will add a few more pages to my booklet. Keeping a record of myself is a lot of fun. It gives me a chance to think about myself. It will be interesting to look back through this book and see how I have grown and changed.

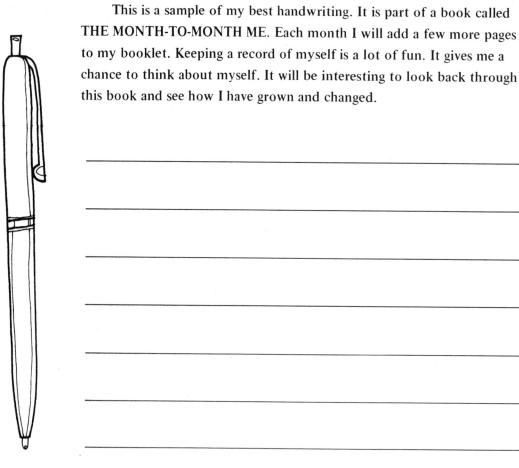

MY GOALS FOR THE YEAR

GOALS AT HOME

1. This year I would like to try and help out more at home by _____

_____ .

2. A new hobby I would like to try this year is _____

_____ .

3. I would like to try and become better at _____

_____ .

4. Another goal of mine at home is _____

_____ .

I'd like to read more books.

AT SCHOOL

1. I would like to try and do better in the area of _____ .

2. This year I would like to become better friends with _____ .

3. One study habit I would like to improve this year is _____

_____ .

4. Another goal of mine at school is _____

_____ .

I'd like to start a stamp collection.

FIRSTS FOR ME

1. word I spoke _____

2. walked alone _____

3. toy _____

4. pet _____

5. friend _____

6. airplane ride _____

7. trip by myself _____

8. prize or award _____

9. loss or defeat _____

10. on stage _____

11. music lesson _____

12. money earned _____

nana!

word

step

toy

pet

friend

ROCKET

music lesson

Lemonade 5¢

money earned

on stage

WINNER HOT DOG EATING CONTEST!

prize or award

MY HOBBIES AND INTERESTS

1. I belong to the following clubs. Place a check (√) by those you belong to and add any which are not listed.

Brownies _____

Blue Birds _____

Campfire Girls _____

Girl Scouts _____

Cub Scouts _____

Boy Scouts _____

Little League _____

School Orchestra _____

School Band _____

School Chorus _____

Chess Club _____

Student Council _____

Church Group _____

Gray Y _____

_____

Others _____

_____

_____

_____

_____

2. I like to collect _____

_____ .

3. If I could have an hour a day at school to study anything I wanted, I would choose:

_____

4. I think it would be fun to learn more about _____ .

5. The things I enjoy doing when I have time to spend just as I please:

at home _____

at school _____

with my friends _____

with my family _____

6. Outside of school I take lessons in _____ .

MY LIKES AND DISLIKES

1. Eight things I really like are:

a. _____   e. _____

b. _____   f. _____

c. _____   g. _____

d. _____   h. _____

guitar music

my dog Fred

skateboarding

sunsets

Disneyland

watering the lawn

chocolate chips

2. Eight things I really dislike are:

a. _____   e. _____

b. _____   f. _____

c. _____   g. _____

d. _____   h. _____

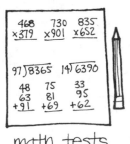

math tests

getting up early

shots

poison oak

liver

spiders

taking out the trash

the smell of cigars

THE STRONG AND WEAK ME

Place a "G" by all the things you are good or strong at. Put a "W" by all the things you are weak at.

science _____

math _____

reading _____

English _____

social studies _____

spelling _____

creative writing _____

handwriting _____

music _____

foreign languages _____

art _____

sports _____

good at sports

being honest _____

being organized _____

being sincere _____

being on time _____

following directions _____

being dependable _____

being courteous _____

self-control _____

finishing what I start _____

taking care of my things _____

paying attention _____

being independent _____

not so good at being on time!

I think my three most important strengths are:

1. _____

2. _____

3. _____

Three areas I want to improve are:

1. _____

2. _____

3. _____

My handwriting could use some improvement!

THE "ING" ME

1. Three "ing" words that best describe me are:

      a. _____

      b. _____

      c. _____

3. Here are pictures of my three "ing" words.

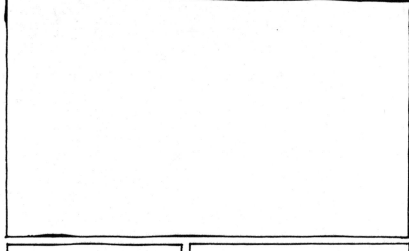

THE REAL ME

The following words describe me best: (Write your answer on the line.)

1. I am more indoor or outdoor _____

2. I am more fast or slow _____

3. I am more past or present _____

4. I am more yes or no _____

5. I am more on the ground or in the air _____

6. I am more a thinker or a doer _____

7. I am more a hamburger or a steak _____

8. I am more a leader or a follower _____

9. I am more a single tree or a forest _____

10. I am more a sports car or a Model-T _____

11. I am more a log cabin or an apartment building _____

12. I am more a frown or a smile _____

13. I am more a morning person or a night person _____

14. I am more an ear or a mouth _____

I am more...
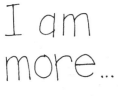 outdoor..
 slow..
 a hamburger..
 a smile..
 a night person

This is how I see myself and how I think others see me. (Use one word for each box.)

	ME	MOM	DAD	FRIEND	TEACHER
NEATNESS					
DEPENDABILITY					
INTELLIGENCE					
HONESTY					
SENSE OF HUMOR					
ATHLETICS					

IN MY OPINION

These are my feelings on the subject of:

1. POLLUTION _____

_____

_____

_____

2. CHEATING _____

_____

_____

_____

3. SMOKING _____

_____

_____

_____

4. STEALING _____

_____

_____

_____

MY MOM

1. My mom's name is _____.

2. She was born in _____ _____.
                              CITY   STATE

3. Some of the different jobs my mom has had are _____

_____.

4. She now works at _____.

5. My mom's hobbies and interests are _____

_____.

6. My mom's favorites

       a. color _____

       b. food _____

       c. sport _____

       d. section of the newspaper _____

       e. kind of book _____

       f. kind of music_____

       g. number _____

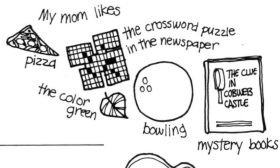

My mom likes the crossword puzzle in the newspaper

pizza

the color green

bowling

THE CLUE IN COBWEB CASTLE

mystery books

folk music

5 the number five

7. The three things I enjoy doing most with my mom are:

_____

_____

_____

I enjoy making cookies with my mom (also eati them)

8. Here is a story about the best time I ever had with my mom. (Use the back of your paper.)

Another thing we like to do together is pull taffy.

December 

MY DAD

1. My dad's name is _____.

2. He was born in _____ _____.
                            CITY   STATE

3. Some of the different jobs my dad has had are _____

_____.

4. He now works at _____.

5. My dad's hobbies and interests are _____

_____.

6. My dad's favorites

    a. color _____

    b. food _____

    c. sport _____

    d. section of the newspaper _____

    e. kind of book _____

    f. kind of music _____

    g. number _____

my dad likes basketball

the front page of the paper

watermelon

banjo music

the number seven

the color red

books about old trains

7. The three things I enjoy doing most with my dad are:

_____

_____

_____

8. Here is a story about the best time I ever had with my dad. (Use the back of your paper.) I enjoy helping my dad work on the car.

My dad and I also enjoy going fishing together.

MY BROTHERS AND SISTERS

1. I have a sister named _____ Age _____

                                 _____ Age _____

                                 _____ Age _____

2. I have a brother named _____ Age _____

                                 _____ Age _____

                                 _____ Age _____

3. The ways in which we are most alike are: _____

_____

4. The ways in which we are most different are: _____

_____

5. Three things I enjoy doing with my brother/sister are:

         a. _____

         b. _____

         c. _____

6. The biggest quarrel I ever had with my brother/sister happened when _____

_____

_____

_____

MY FAMILY SHIELD

1. In box 1 is a picture of the people in my family.

2. In box 2 is a picture of something my family enjoys doing together.

3. In box 3 is a picture of some place I have traveled or visited with my family.

4. In box 4 is a picture of my house.

5. In box 5 is a picture of my pet.

6. In box 6 is a picture of one of my favorite relatives. (grandparent, aunt, uncle, cousin, etc.)

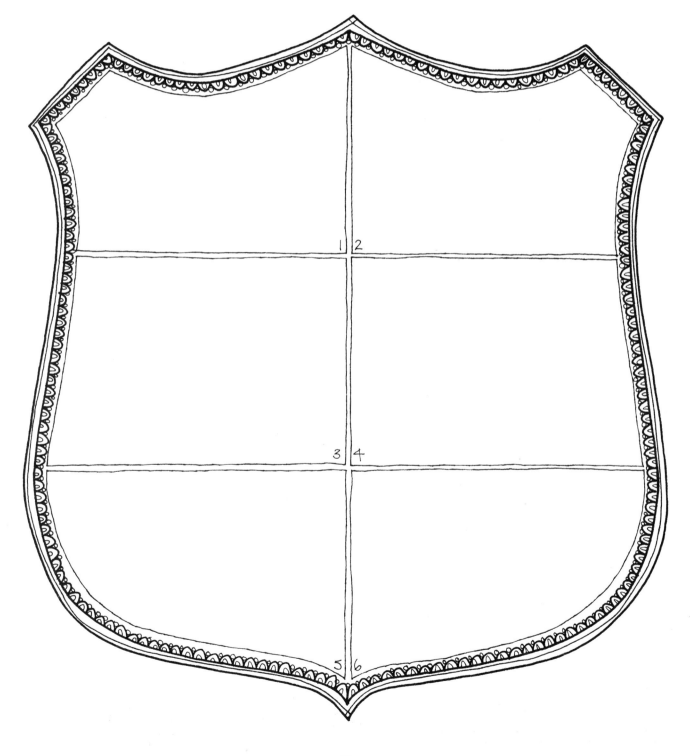

A MAP TO SCHOOL

Here is a map showing how to get from my house to school. (Be sure to fill in street names.)

(Use these symbols on your map.)

house –   school – 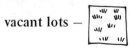   trees – 🌳🌳🌳🌳   apartment –

vacant lots –

FACTS ABOUT MY SCHOOL

1. The name of my school is _____ .

2. The address of my school is _____ .

3. This year I am in the _____ grade. My teacher's name is _____ .

    I am in room _____ .

    I am in room 42.

4. I have been going to this school for _____ years.

5. The principal of my school is _____ .

6. Our school secretary is _____ .

7. The name of the school nurse is _____ .

8. Our school custodian is _____ .

9. One thing I like about my school is _____

    _____ .

10. One thing I dislike about my school is _____

    _____ .

11. Here is a picture of the front of my school.

MY TEACHER

(Interview your teacher and find these statements.)

1. My teacher's name is _____ .

2. He/she was born in _____ .

3. Some of the different jobs my teacher has had are _____

_____ .

4. My teacher's hobbies and interests are _____

_____ .

5. My teacher's favorites

    a. color   _____

    b. food   _____

    c. sport   _____

    d. section of the newspaper _____

    e. kind of book _____

    f. kind of music _____

    g. number   _____

My teacher likes:
the color yellow
tennis
hot fudge sundaes
classical music
MOZART
PERU
books about other countries
OPINION — the editorial page
the number one hundred 100

6. Here is a story about one thing that happened this year between my teacher and me that I will never forget. (Use the back of your paper.)

I'll never forget the time my art teacher said I should think about being a professional artist.

THOUGHTS ABOUT SCHOOL

1. I think school _____.

2. I think my school work _____.

3. My favorite subjects in school are _____

_____

_____.

4. My least favorite subjects in school are _____

_____

_____.

5. The funniest thing that happened to me in school this year was _____

_____

_____.

6. The most embarrassing thing that happened to me in school this year was _____

_____

_____.

7. The best day I had at school this year was when _____

_____.

8. The worst day I had at school this year was when _____

_____.

The worst day I had at school this year was when I fell down in the cafeteria and spilled everything on my tray.

FRIENDSHIP

1. I am happy when a friend _____

   _____ .

2. I am unhappy when a friend _____

   _____ .

3. I think it is important for a friend to be _____

   _____ .

4. I enjoy talking to my friends about _____ .

5. One nice thing I have done for a friend is _____

   _____ .

6. One nice thing a friend has done for me is _____

   _____ .

7. Sometimes my friends make me _____

8. My friends think I am _____ .

9. Here is a story about a special time I shared with a friend. (Use the back of your paper.)

FUN WITH MY FRIENDS

1. The things I enjoy doing with my friends are:

    a. _____

    b. _____

    c. _____

    d. _____

    e. _____

    f. _____

2. The best time I ever had with a friend was _____

_____

_____ .

3. The worst disagreement I ever had with a friend was _____

_____

_____ .

I enjoy putting on puppet shows with my friends.

WHAT IS A FRIEND?

I think it is important for a friend to be:

(Place a number 1 by the one you feel is most important; a number 2 by the next most important, etc.)

1. ATHLETIC _____

2. CHEERFUL _____

3. CREATIVE _____

4. CLEAN _____

5. FORGIVING _____

6. HELPFUL _____

7. POLITE _____

8. SMART _____

9. TRUTHFUL _____

10. UNDERSTANDING _____

smart

cheerful

athletic

polite

helpful

PICTURES OF MY FRIENDS

Here are pictures of my best friends.

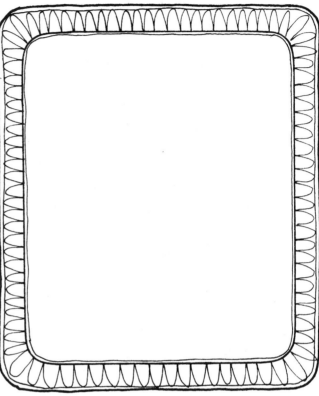

Name _____

Name _____

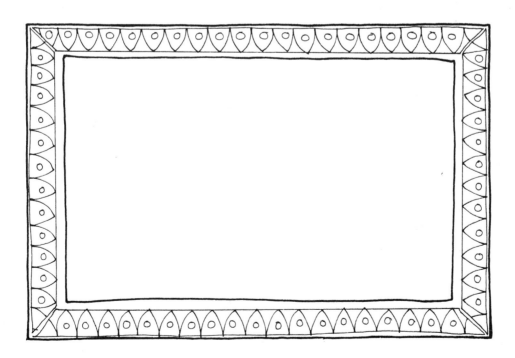

Name _____

MY ALL-TIME FAVORITES

These are my all-time favorites

1. number _____
2. color _____
3. school subject _____
4. animal _____
5. flower _____
6. song _____
7. television show _____
8. time of the day _____
9. day of the week _____
10. month of the year _____
11. game to play _____
12. place to visit _____
13. sport _____
14. friends _____
15. holiday _____
16. section of the newspaper _____
17. movie _____
18. car _____
19. restaurant _____
20. recording group _____
21. actor/actress _____
22. athlete _____
23. teacher _____
24. comic strip character _____
25. thing to wear _____

number

color

school subject

animal

flower

television program

time of day

month JULY

day of week

game to play

thing to wear

recording group

sport

MY FAVORITE FOODS

1. If I could plan a special meal, this is what my menu would look like:

SOUP _____

SALAD _____

MAIN COURSE _____

2 VEGETABLES _____

_____

DESSERT _____

DRINK _____

2. Other favorite foods:

a. meat _____

b. fish _____

c. fruit _____

d. vegetable _____

e. cereal _____

f. egg dish _____

g. soup _____

h. ice-cream _____

i. candy _____

j. cake _____

k. cookie _____

l. bread _____

MY FAVORITE BOOK

1. I do _____ do not _____ enjoy reading books. (Check one.)

2. I do _____ do not _____ like having someone read to me. (Check one.)

3. I spend about _____ each day reading books at home.

4. I get books from the library every _____ .

5. Some books I own are _____

_____ .

6. My favorite book is _____ .

7. The main character in my favorite book is _____ .

8. The story is about _____

_____

_____

9. Here is a picture of the cover of my favorite book. (Be sure to include the title and author.)

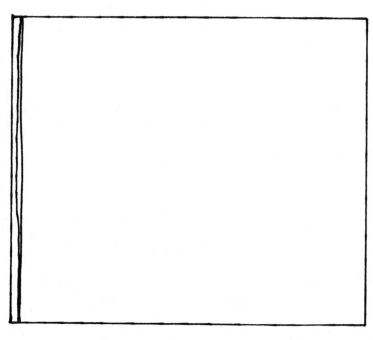
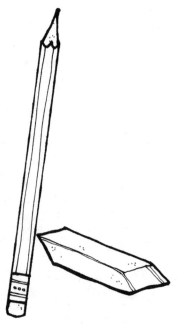

PICTURE FAVORITES

Here are pictures of my favorite . . .

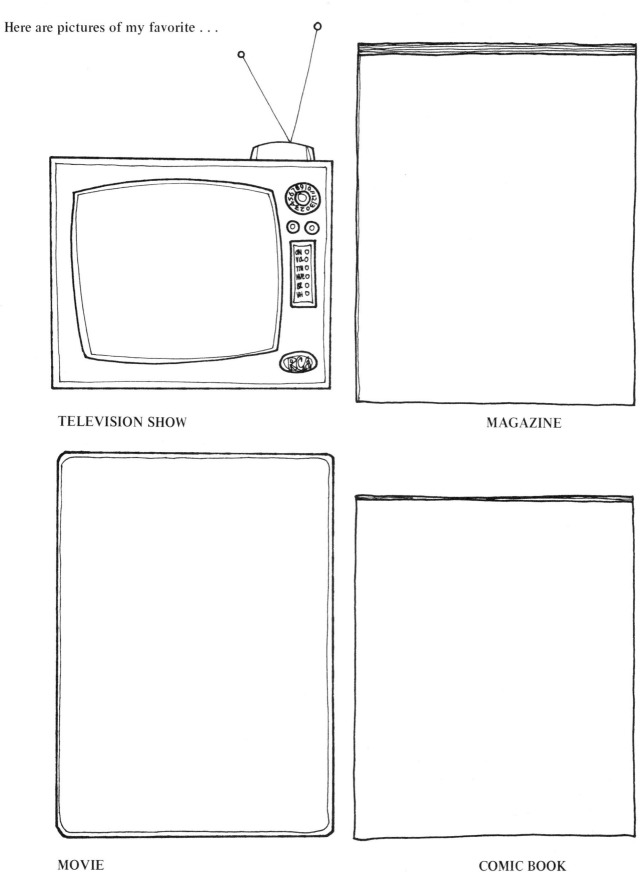

TELEVISION SHOW

MAGAZINE

MOVIE

COMIC BOOK

MY FEELINGS

These are a few sentences telling about one time I felt very . . .

1. EXCITED _____
_____
_____

2. LOVED _____
_____
_____

3. JEALOUS _____
_____
_____

4. LONELY _____
_____
_____

5. FRIGHTENED _____
_____
_____

THE HAPPY ME ☺

1. The touch of _____ makes me happy.

2. The sight of _____ makes me happy.

3. The sound of _____ makes me happy.

4. The smell of _____ makes me happy.

5. The taste of _____ makes me happy.

6. I am most happy when I am _____

_____

_____ .

7. This is a story of one of the happiest days I can remember.

_____

_____

_____

_____

_____

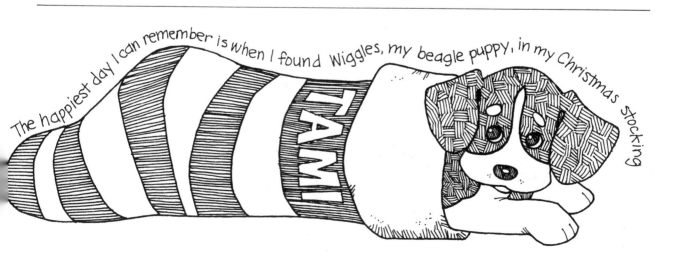

The happiest day I can remember is when I found Wiggles, my beagle puppy, in my Christmas stocking

THE SAD ME :(

1. The touch of _____ makes me sad.

2. The sight of _____ makes me sad.

3. The sound of _____ makes me sad.

4. The smell of _____ makes me sad.

5. The taste of _____ makes me sad.

6. I feel sad when _____

_____

_____.

7. This is a story of one of the saddest days I can remember.

_____

_____

_____

_____

_____

THE ANGRY ME

1. Three things that really make me mad are:

   a. _____

   b. _____

   c. _____

2. When I lose my temper I _____

   _____ .

3. Here is a story about one time I got very angry. (How did it start? Who did it involve? How did you handle it?)

   _____

   _____

   _____

   _____

   _____

   _____

WHAT IF?

1. If I could be any person in the world I would be _____

   because _____ .

2. If I could be an animal I would be a/an _____

   because _____ .

3. If I could live during any period of time in history I would choose _____

   _____ because _____ .

4. If I could live in any city in the United States I would choose _____

   because _____ .

5. If I could change one thing about myself, it would be _____

   because _____ .

6. If I could have any talent I wanted I would choose _____

   because _____ .

7. If I had all the money I wanted I would _____

   because _____ .

8. If I could make one wish for the world it would be _____

   _____ because _____ .

9. Here is a picture of one of my "if's."

MY TRAVEL PLANS

1. I have visited the following places: (Place a check (√) by those you have visited.)

a. _____ airport

b. _____ amusement park

c. _____ art gallery

d. _____ ball game

e. _____ beach

f. _____ circus

g. _____ museum

h. _____ observatory

i. _____ planetarium

j. _____ plant or factory

k. _____ zoo

l. _____

2. I have visited the following states:

_____

_____

3. I have visited the following foreign countries: _____

_____

4. In the future I would like to visit these three places:

a. _____ b. _____ c. _____

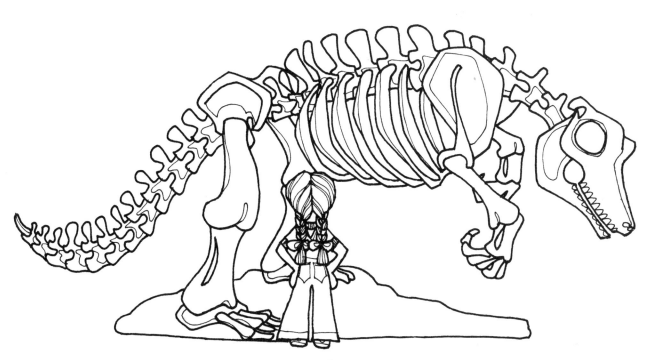

WORK IN THE FUTURE

1. In the future I would like to work (check one.)

    a. indoors _____ outdoors _____

    b. at night _____ during the day _____

    c. with people _____ on machines _____

    d. with children _____ with adults _____ with animals _____

    e. sitting at a desk _____ standing on my feet _____

    f. wearing a uniform _____ without a uniform _____

WITH PEOPLE
OUTDOORS
WITH ANIMALS TOO
STANDING ON MY FEET

2. I have thought about the following occupations: _____

_____ because I am good at _____ .

3. I will need the following training or education for this occupation:

_____

_____

_____

4. An advantage of this occupation is _____ .

5. A disadvantage of this occupation is _____ .

6. Here is a picture of me working on my job.

MY CRYSTAL BALL

Gazing into my crystal ball, here are pictures of what I see.

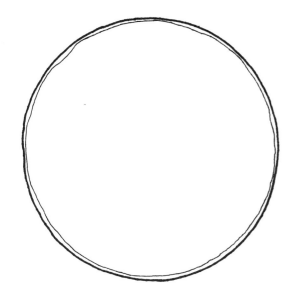

1. Next year I see myself:

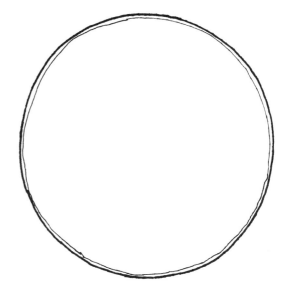

2. In five years I see myself:

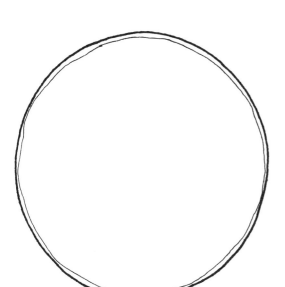

3. In ten years I see myself:

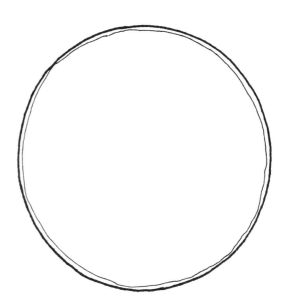

4. In fifteen years I see myself:

A SELF PORTRAIT

This is how I think I look at the end of the school year.

Draw your picture here. Compare this picture with the one you drew at the beginning of the school year. How do you think you have changed?

MY HANDWRITING

This is a sample of my best handwriting. (Compare this page with your handwriting at the beginning of the school year.)

COPY THIS PARAGRAPH.

> This is a sample of my best handwriting. It is part of a book called THE MONTH-TO-MONTH ME. Each month I added a few more pages to my booklet. Keeping a record of myself was a lot of fun. It gave me a chance to think about myself. It is interesting to look back through this book and see how I have grown and changed.

_____

_____

_____

_____

_____

_____

MY SUMMER PLANS

1. This summer I plan to visit _____

    _____ .

2. Two books I would like to read this summer are _____

    _____

    _____ .

3. One new sport I would like to try this summer is _____ .

4. A new hobby or interest I am interested in learning or starting this summer is _____

    _____ .

5. This summer I am going to try and _____

    _____ .

6. This summer I would really like to see _____

    _____ .

7. Here is a picture of one thing I want to do this summer . . .

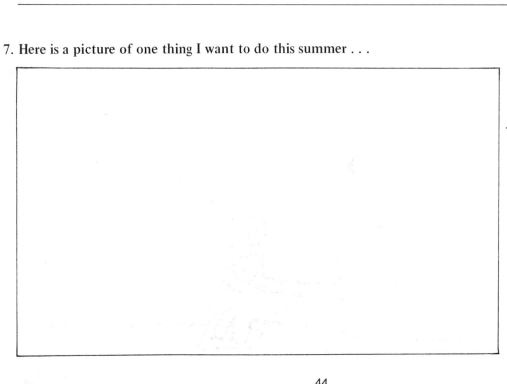

WHAT I'VE LEARNED ABOUT MYSELF

1. I met the following goals I set for myself on Page 9:

_____

_____

2. In comparing my two portraits, I have changed by _____

_____ .

3. In comparing the two samples of my handwriting, I think my handwriting has changed by _____

_____ .

4. In looking over THE MONTH-TO-MONTH ME, I learned that I _____

_____

_____ .

5. I never realized that I _____

_____ .

6. I was happy that I _____

_____ .

7. I was disappointed _____

_____ .

8. I think I have made the biggest improvement in _____

_____ .

Autographs
of fine friends and famous folks

AUTO GRAPHS...

PRINTS
OF AN AUTOGRAPH
HOUND